The Birthplace of Stars

T0061952

Mari Bolte

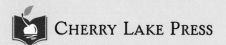

CHERRY LAKE PRESS

Published in the United States of America by Cherry Lake Publishing Group
Ann Arbor, Michigan
www.cherrylakepublishing.com

Reading Adviser: Beth Walker Gambro, MS, Ed., Reading Consultant, Yorkville, IL
Content Adviser: Robert S. Kowalczyk, MS, Physics, Systems Engineer (Retired) at the NASA Jet Propulsion Laboratory

Photo Credits: page 1: ©Blueee77/Shutterstock; page 5: ©Suchart Kuathan/Getty Images; page 6: ©Pakin Songmor/Getty Images; page 9: ©Robert Gendler/Stocktrek Images/Getty Images; page 10: ©NASA, ESA, CSA, STScI/flickr.com; page 12: ©muratart/Shutterstock; page 15: ©MARK GARLICK/SCIENCE PHOTO LIBRARY/Getty Images; page 16: ©NASA, ESA, CSA, STScI/flickr.com; page 19: ©Outer Space/Shutterstock; page 20: ©NASA, ESA, CSA, STScI, Megan Reiter (Rice University), with image processing by Joseph DePasquale (STScI), Anton M. Koekemoer (STScI)/flickr.com; page 22: ©Tragoolchitr Jittasaiyapan/Shutterstock; page 23: ©Sansanorth/Shutterstock; page 25: ©ESA/Hubble & NASA, C. Murray, E. Sabbi; Acknowledgment: Y.-H. Chu/nasa.gov; page 26: ©X-ray: NASA/CXC/Penn State Univ./L. Townsley et al.; IR: NASA/ESA/CSA/STScI/JWST ERO Production Team/flickr.com; page 28: ©alionaprof/Shutterstock

Library of Congress Cataloging-in-Publication Data
Cataloging-in-Publication Data has been filed and is available at catalog.loc.gov.

ISBN 9781668938386 Lib.

Cherry Lake Publishing Group would like to acknowledge the work of the Partnership for 21st Century Learning, a Network of Battelle for Kids. Please visit Battelle for Kids online for more information.

Note from publisher: Websites change regularly, and their future contents are outside of our control. Supervise children when conducting any recommended online searches for extended learning opportunities.

Printed in the United States of America

Mari Bolte is an author and editor of children's books in every subject imaginable. She hopes the next generation sets their sights on the sky and beyond. Never stop the love of learning!

CONTENTS

CHAPTER 1

Born in the Clouds

When you look up at the night sky, the stars seem to stretch on forever. What you see is very similar to what people saw 2,000 years ago. People living 2,000 years from now will be able to do the same thing.

Those stars didn't just appear, though. They were born. They live. And then they die. A star's life is much longer than ours. Some of the shortest-lived stars live around 10 million years. The oldest known star is 12 billion years old.

Stars are born inside clouds of space dust called nebulae. This dust is different from dust on Earth. Space dust is made up of solid bits from comets, asteroids, and other objects that move around in space. Gravity pulls those bits together into a **mass**. It becomes **dense** and hot. It reaches 59 million degrees Fahrenheit (33 million degrees Celsius). Then it's officially a star.

There are around 200 billion trillion stars in the universe. That's a 2 with 23 zeros after it!

There is a lot we don't know about how stars are born. The *James Webb Space Telescope* is helping us learn more. Its high-powered cameras have captured never-before-seen views of what goes on inside the birthplaces of stars.

Milky Way Facts

Our galaxy, the Milky Way, forms about seven new stars EVERY YEAR.

We can see about 600 stars from Earth without a telescope. But the Milky Way alone has more than 100 BILLION stars.

Ancient Roman astronomers called the Milky Way the "ROAD MADE OF MILK."

CHAPTER 2

The Pillars of Creation

In 1995, the *Hubble Space Telescope* sent NASA scientists an amazing image. Three tall towers looked like rock. They stretched across the sky. These towers aren't rock, though. They are very dense clouds of gas and space dust. Inside the clouds are new stars. Scientists named the towers the Pillars of Creation.

Hubble took an even clearer image in 2014 to honor that first discovery. Seven years later, the *James Webb Space Telescope* launched from Earth. It settled into its orbit around the Sun in January 2022. The telescope's first image was shown to the public that July. And in October, the world got to see something even more amazing. *Webb* had taken the clearest image ever of the Pillars of Creation.

The Eagle Nebula is also known as Messier 16. Charles Messier was a French astronomer. He cataloged over 100 space objects in the 1700s.

The pillars are part of the Eagle Nebula. The nebula is about 7,000 light-years away. One light-year is about 5.9 trillion miles (9.5 trillion kilometers). It can be seen through a regular telescope on Earth. During a dark summer night, look to the northern sky. Find the Serpens constellation. The nebula is part of it.

The Eagle Nebula measures 70 by 55 light-years in area. The pillars look small inside the nebula. But they are 4 to 5 light-years in size. That's larger than our entire solar system!

Newly formed stars appear as BRIGHT RED spiky orbs just outside the pillars.

Even the WEBB TELESCOPE cannot peer through the pillars' densest, darkest areas of space dust.

Pillars of Creation Facts

The wavy lines along some of the pillar edges are JETS OF ENERGY that shoot out from new stars. The **supersonic** jets hit clouds and create shockwaves.

Comets are one source of space dust.

Webb's Near-Infrared Camera (NIRCam) can see through a lot of space dust. It shows us much of what's inside the Pillars of Creation. Infrared light has longer wavelengths than visible light. This means the light can pass through space dust. The dust then looks transparent in pictures. Objects that were once hidden are now visible.

Take a closer look at the Pillars of Creation image. There are no visible galaxies. Scientists would usually expect to see them. But dense dust blocks their light even from *Webb*'s infrared sensors. Between every star is something called interstellar medium. This is a mix of hydrogen and helium gas, with some solid bits of dust. Even if the medium is thin in some places, the amount between two stars that are far apart adds up. Think about a sheet of tissue paper. One sheet is thin and easy to rip through. You can even see light on the other side. But that changes if you stack many sheets on top of each other.

Around 15 percent of visible matter in the Milky Way is interstellar medium. This is why we can't see faraway galaxies through the Pillars of Creation. NIRCam can see through the nearest layers. But eventually, the layers become too thick to see beyond that.

INTERNATIONAL OBSERVATION

Unveiling the secrets of the universe is a team effort. More than 100 scientists from all over the world are working together. They study how the birth of new stars changes the local nebulae. This team is called Physics at High Angular Resolution in Nearby Galaxies (PHANGS). They study images taken by many telescopes and scientific tools called instruments.

One of those instruments is the *Atacama Large Millimeter/ Submillimeter Array (ALMA)* in Chile. *ALMA* showed the gases present in star formation. Another telescope in Chile, the *Very Large Telescope*, was also used. One of its instruments showed late-stage star formation. *Hubble* added visible and **ultraviolet** light images. They showed stars and star clusters. Because *Webb* can see past space dust, its data helps fill in some of the blanks about how stars are born.

CHAPTER 3

The Fiery Hourglass

Interstellar medium surrounds everything in space. In some places, it's thin and barely there. In others, it collects into big nebula clouds. The clouds can be enormous. Some are hundreds of light-years across. Gravity increases inside the nebula clouds. It begins to pull the gases into a ball. The ball forms a **protostar**. *Proto* means "first" or "original."

In November 2022, the *James Webb Space Telescope* turned the clock back in time. It sent back an image of a nebula called L1527. This nebula is around 460 light-years away. It looks as though it is being pinched in the center, forming an hourglass shape. This unique nebula has a fiery appearance. It is from the object in its center—a protostar. Material is being pulled toward the new star, creating the curving lines.

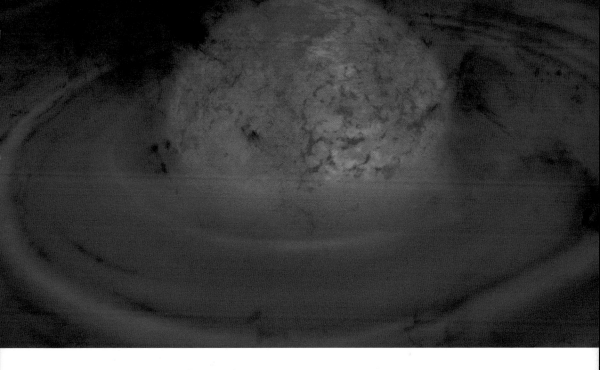

This artist's rendition shows the gas and dust that surround a protostar and hide it from visible light.

L1527's protostar is only 100 thousand years old. It could take another 400 to 900 thousand years for the protostar to reach the next stage in its life. Currently, it is only 20 to 40 percent as large as our Sun. The protostar is so small, it can't even be seen yet. A dark line crossing the center of the hourglass can be seen, though. It is from a ring-shaped disk of matter. The disk surrounds the protostar. Its material might form into planets around the new star.

The birthing PROTOSTAR'S LIGHT illuminates the dust and gas on either side of the disk.

L1527 Facts

The bubble shapes in the top half of the hourglass are created by STELLAR "BURPS." They are caused by the protostar feeding heavily on nearby gas and dust.

Reddish strings in the bottom half of the hourglass are caused by SHOCKWAVES. The disruption prevents other stars from forming.

CHAPTER 4

Among the Cosmic Cliffs

People living in the Southern Hemisphere can see the constellation Carina. There is an interstellar nursery inside it. It's around 7,600 light-years from us. One of the first photos *Webb* sent back was of the interior of the Carina Nebula. It appears like there are mountains and valleys inside the nebula. They are called the Cosmic Cliffs. This area is also known as NGC 3324.

The cliffs are at the edge of a "canyon" inside the nebula. The nebula's wall is being scraped away by ultraviolet **radiation** and **stellar wind**. These forces are created by extremely hot, young stars. They sit just outside the top of *Webb*'s picture.

Carina is one of the largest and brightest nebulae in the Milky Way.

NASA scientists now think that there are at least 24 previously unknown protostars inside the Cosmic Cliffs. These young stars spew out jets of leftover gas and dust. *Webb*'s photo is the first time this stage of star birth has been seen. In the past, *Hubble* was only able to see jets from older stars. But *Webb*'s extra-sensitive cameras are able to pick up this short-lived stage of the stellar life cycle. Many of these new stars are expected to grow into stars like our Sun.

Cosmic Cliffs Facts

The highest cliffs stand around 7 LIGHT-YEARS tall. They are holding up against fierce stellar winds.

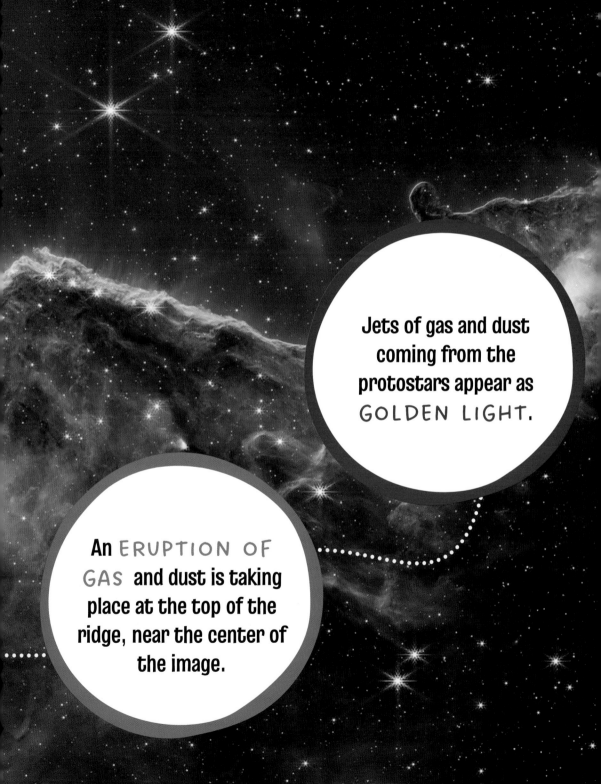

Jets of gas and dust coming from the protostars appear as GOLDEN LIGHT.

An ERUPTION OF GAS and dust is taking place at the top of the ridge, near the center of the image.

The Andromeda Galaxy is a large, spiral-shaped galaxy, just like the Milky Way.

Scientists have been studying nebulae such as NGC 3324 for hundreds of years. The first nebula ever seen was Messier 27. It was discovered in 1764. James Dunlop was the first to see NGC 3324. He saw it in 1826 through a small telescope.

Astronomer Edwin Hubble later turned a telescope toward our nearest neighbor, the Andromeda Galaxy, in 1924. It was once known as the Andromeda Nebula. Scientists used to think it was part of the Milky Way. But Edwin Hubble was able to see that some nebulae were outside our galaxy.

In 2015, the *Hubble Space Telescope* sent back the sharpest view of Andromeda ever taken. More than 100 million stars were shown inside a 61,000-light-year stretch of sky. NASA compared it to taking a picture of a beach and being able

Lenses and Light

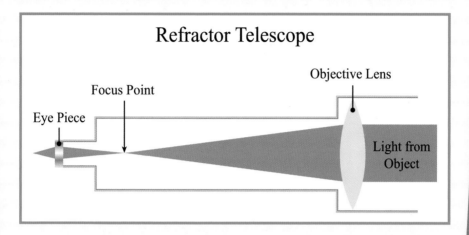

Refractor Telescope

Objective Lens

Focus Point

Eye Piece

Light from Object

The first telescopes were invented in 1608. Inventors used curved pieces of glass. They make faraway objects look closer. Today, most telescopes use curved mirrors instead. The curve focuses light that comes from outer space. The most powerful telescopes can gather a lot of light.

The larger the mirror, the more light the telescope can collect. *Hubble* uses two mirrors to collect and focus light. The main mirror is 7.8 feet (2.4 meters) across. *Webb* uses 18 mirrors. Together, they are 21.3 feet (6.5 m) wide. It is the largest mirror ever launched into space.

to see individual grains of sand. Technological advances, like the *Hubble* and *Webb* telescopes, put our tiny planet into perspective. Brand-new images of outer space will only get clearer as telescope technology gets better and better.

CHAPTER 5

Caught in a Webb

Only 161,000 light-years away is an enormous gathering of stars. It's inside the Tarantula Nebula, also known as 30 Doradus. It was discovered in the early 1750s. It is the largest and brightest star-forming nebula near the Milky Way.

Modern-day scientists have explored this stellar nursery for many years. *Hubble* showed that 30 Doradus creates stars incredibly fast. Scientists were able to see protostars just a few thousand years old. They also saw huge stars that grew fast and died young.

Viewed through *Webb*'s NIRCam, the nebula looks like the home of a burrowing tarantula. The "silk" that lines the burrow is from gas and dust. The "silk" is blown away by radiation. A giant bright blue cluster sits in the center. For years, scientists believed it was one big star. Now they

Over the years, space telescopes have taken many photographs of the Tarantula Nebula.

know that it's made up of around 500,000 protostars. At its very core are eight enormous stars. Each is around 100 times more massive than the Sun. They are also around 10 times hotter.

Star birth has been seen in many different galaxies. But the Tarantula Nebula is relatively near to Earth. Scientists can study it up close and in great detail.

Tarantula Nebula Facts

Radiation from the bright blue cluster of protostars has created a hole in the cloud of dust—the TARANTULA'S "BURROW."

The areas surrounding these stars are DENSE PILLARS. Protostars are being created there.

An ancient mix of chemicals, similar to when the universe was only a few billion years old, makes up the TARANTULA NEBULA.

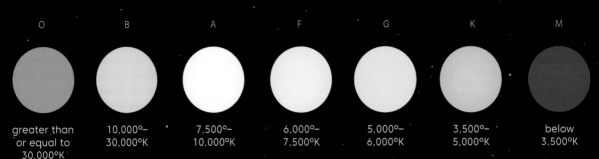

O	B	A	F	G	K	M
greater than or equal to 30,000°K	10,000°– 30,000°K	7,500°– 10,000°K	6,000°– 7,500°K	5,000°– 6,000°K	3,500°– 5,000°K	below 3,500°K

Temperature

The Harvard Spectral Classification divides stars based on how hot they are. Their temperatures are marked in Kelvin. This is the standard unit of measuring heat at very low or very high temperatures.

The way a star is born affects the rest of its life. The cloud of dust that creates protostars spins as it collapses into a mass. It ends up forming a disk around the protostar. Sometimes, the disks become planets and moons. Smaller protostars can take more than 100 million years to emerge. Massive stars live and die faster. If the cloud of dust fails to become massive enough to burn hot, the star fails. These failed protostars are called brown dwarfs.

Stars are classified by their **spectral** characteristics. This is how hot they burn. The star's temperature also determines the star's color. Stars are labeled O, B, A, F, G, K, or M. O stars are the hottest. M are the coolest. Our Sun is a G star.

Scientists want to learn more about how protostars are created. Finding out how they become stars and learning more about their life cycles is key to understanding our own galaxy. Joel Green is a scientist at the Space Telescope Science Institute. He said, "Planets are essentially the crumbs that don't end up in a star." If we can trace those crumbs, we might even find alien worlds that are as full of life as our own.

WHAT'S IN A NAME?

Naming things helps scientists keep track of them. But one thing might have many different names. For example, the brightest star in the night sky is most commonly called Sirius. That means "glowing" in Greek. But it's also known as the Dog Star. Chinese, Sanskrit, Latin, Arabic, and other astronomers gave it their own names.

In 2016, a list of approved star names was released by a group of astronomers. The first batch included well-known bright stars. For example, one star's name had been spelled more than 30 different ways throughout history. A single spelling was agreed upon: Fomalhaut. The scientists hoped that doing this would help avoid confusion in the future.

Space objects are also given official scientific names. The Harry Draper Catalogue (HD) gives each star a number. The numbers tell scientists where it is located in the sky. For example, Sirius is HD 48915. Galaxies, nebulae, and star clusters are given NGC numbers. They are part of the New General Catalogue.

Activity

Connect to STEAM: Engineering

The *James Webb Space Telescope* cost billions of dollars to build. Personal telescopes can range in price from hundreds to thousands of dollars. You don't need to make a trip to the store in order to look at the deep sky, though. Try your hand at engineering your very own telescope.

MATERIALS NEEDED

- a helpful adult
- two empty paper towel tubes
- scissors
- clear tape
- reading glasses with at least 2x magnification

1. Pick a tube to be the inner tube. Cut it down the long side. Overlap the edges on one end and hold them together while you push that end into the outer tube. Let go so it unravels inside the outer tube. Leave one edge of the inner tube sticking out a bit.

2. Remove the lenses from the glasses. Tape one lens onto the edge of the inner tube. The lens should curve out. Try not to cover too much of it with tape.

3. Now attach a lens to the other end. This time, tape it to the edge of the outer tube, with the lens curving out.

4. Look at something through the inner tube's lens. Slide the inner tube in and out until the image is focused. Because your telescope has two lenses, images appear upside-down. Many telescopes work this way.

5. Decorate your telescope using paint, markers, or colored pencils. Enjoy looking at faraway objects during the day or at night!

Find Out More

Books

Bolte, Mari. *Mysteries Revealed*. Ann Arbor, MI: Cherry Lake Publishing, 2024.

Langley, Andrew. *Space Telescopes: Instagram of the Stars*. North Mankato, MN: Capstone Press, 2019.

Rossiter, Brienna. *Big Machines in Space*. Lake Elmo, MN: Focus Readers, 2021.

Stratton, Connor. *Space Exploration*. Lake Elmo, MN: Focus Readers, 2023.

Online Resources to Search with an Adult

JWST: Where Is *Webb*?

Kiddle: *James Webb Space Telescope* Facts for Kids

Webb Space Telescope: The Beginning of Everything

WorldAtlas: What Is a Star Nursery?

Glossary

dense (DENS) very thick and heavy

infrared (in-fruh-RED) invisible light from beyond the red end of the visible light spectrum

light-years (LYTE-YEERZ) units of distance equal to how far light travels in 1 year—6 trillion miles (9.6 trillion km)

mass (MAS) a collection of matter combined through forces of gravity

medium (MEE-dee-uhm) material that makes up a particular environment

protostar (PROH-toh-stahr) a very young star that is still forming

radiation (ray-dee-AY-shuhn) energy that comes from a source in the form of waves or rays you cannot see

spectral (SPEK-truhl) having to do with the spectrum of colors that a ray of light can be separated into: red, orange, yellow, green, blue, indigo, and violet

stellar wind (STEH-luhr WIND) fast flows of gas and tiny particles that are ejected from stars

supersonic (soo-puhr-SAH-nik) faster than the speed of sound

ultraviolet (uhl-truh-VIE-luht) invisible light from the violet end of the light spectrum

wavelengths (WAYV-lengths) measurements between one wave to another as energy flows through space in a wavelike pattern

Index